THE MUSEUM OF THE CITY OF NEW YORK
Portraits of America

Coney Island

John S. Berman

D1297003

BARNES
&NOBLE
BOOKS
NEW YORK

A BARNES & NOBLE BOOK

© 2003 Barnes & Noble Publishing, Inc.

Library of Congress Cataloging-in-Publication Data

Berman, John S.

    Coney Island / John S. Berman.
      p. cm. -- (Portraits of America)
    ISBN 0-7607-3887-4 (alk. paper)
    1. Coney Island (New York, N.Y.)--History. 2. Amusement parks--New York (State)--New York--History. 3. New York (N.Y.)--History. I. Title. II. Series.

    F129.C75 B47 2002
    974.7'23--dc21

                                    2002034299

Editor: Rosy Ngo
Art Director: Kevin Ullrich
Designer: Liz Trovato
Photography Editor: Lori Epstein
Digital Imaging: Daniel J. Rutkowski
Production Manager: Richela Fabian Morgan

Color separations by Bright Arts Graphics (S) Pte Ltd.
Printed and bound in China by C&C Offset Printing Co. Ltd.

10 9 8 7 6 5 4 3 2 1

About the Museum of the City of New York

The Museum of the City of New York is one of New York City's great cultural treasures—the first U.S. museum dedicated to the study of a single city. Founded in 1923, it presents the nearly four hundred–year evolution of one of history's most important metropolises through exhibitions, educational programs, and publications, and by collecting and preserving the artifacts that tell New York's remarkable stories.

The Museum's collection of 1.5 million objects reflects the diverse and dramatic history of New York City. In addition to prints and photographs, the Museum collects and preserves paintings and sculptures, costumes, theater memorabilia, decorative arts and furniture, police and fire fighting materials, toys made or used in New York, material related to the history of the port, and thousands of varied objects and documents that illuminate the lives of New Yorkers, past and present. Among the gems of the collections are gowns worn at George Washington's inaugural ball, New York's last surviving omnibus and one of its last Checker Cabs, archives of the work of renowned photographers Jacob A. Riis and Berenice Abbott, the world's largest collection of Currier & Ives prints, and pieces of the Times Square news "zipper."

Through its Department of Learning, the Museum offers programs to thousands of teachers and students from all five boroughs every year, including guided tours, teacher training, and its annual New York City History Day contest— the nation's largest urban history fair. Other activities for audiences of all ages include hands-on workshops, performances, book readings, scholarly conferences and lectures, films, and walking tours.

The Museum's rich collections and archives are available to the public for research. To learn how to explore the collections or how to order reproductions of images, visit the Museum's website at www.mcny.org. The website also features exhibition previews, up-to-date program information, an on-line Museum shop, virtual exhibitions, student aids, and information on how you can support the Museum's work.

MUSEUM OF THE
CITY OF NEW YORK
1220 Fifth Avenue
New York, NY 10029
(212) 534-1672
www.mcny.org

Contents

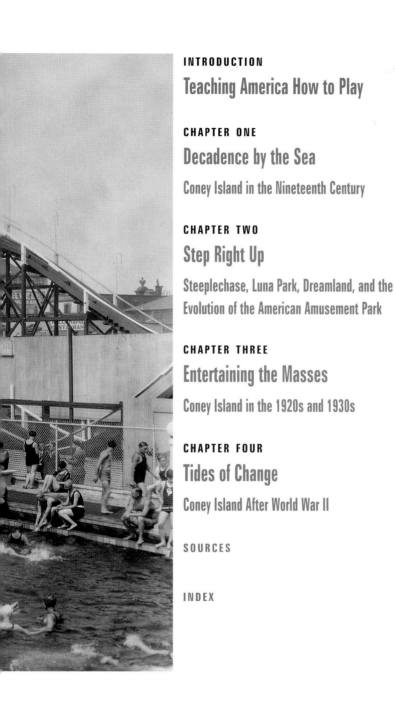

Above: Surf Avenue is generally considered to be Coney Island's main drag. In this 1905 photo, we can see what passed for a traffic jam in the days of horse-drawn carriages, and how men of this era tended to favor the same kind of hat.

Teaching America How to Play

"It is blatant, it is cheap, it is the apotheosis of the ridiculous but is something more. It is like Niagara Falls or the Grand Canyon or Yellowstone Park. It is a national playground and not to have seen it is not to have seen your own country."

So spoke Reginald Wright Kaufman in 1909. And anyone in America during the early years of the twentieth century would have known exactly what he was talking about. There was only one Coney Island and only one summertime destination for tens of thousands of New Yorkers. Each year these city denizens sought to leave behind real-life worries and lose themselves in the wild thrills of the amusement parks—Luna Park, Steeplechase Park, and Dreamland—or to pass long summer days on the beaches with friends. Coney Island was the place to get Nathan's Famous hot dogs and ride the Cyclone. There were freak shows and wild rides—the Loop the Loop, the Razzle Dazzle, and the Shoot the Chutes—dance pavilions, and the boardwalk. It was a place for first kisses and first dates, diversion and flirtation. It was spectacular, unpredictable, and a little risky; grotesque and tawdry; full of forbidden pleasures and magical adventures. Coney Island embodied youth culture in the days before hot rods and shopping malls; its attractions defined leisure activities before television and video games.

Coney Island is the single most famous beach resort and amusement park in United States history, and its carefree spirit symbolizes the enormous transformation that took place in the society and culture of New York City during the late nineteenth and early twentieth centuries. In many respects, the popular amusements found at Coney Island exemplified the movement away from Victorian refinement and the shaping of a new "mass culture" in America. The sharp decline of the once-bright resort in the second half of the twentieth century can also be seen as emblematic of the decay of New York City and other urban communities. Quite a colorful history for Coney Island—a small spit of land at the end of Brooklyn that was never really an island at all.

Above: The idea of the beach as a place to spend the day began to take hold among New Yorkers in the first three decades of the twentieth century. This photograph, circa 1908, shows a number of people enjoying the sand and sea.

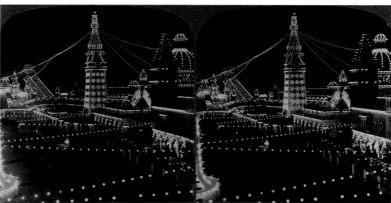

Above: Luna Park was at its most spectacular at night, when beams of light radiated from the many tower steeples. In stereoscope this image springs to life.

Above: A quintessential wartime photograph shows a sailor and his girlfriend eating from the same Coney Island hot dog in 1943.

Above: Hot dog king Nathan Handwerker began his Coney Island career in 1915 working in the restaurant owned by Charles Feltman, who is usually credited with "inventing" the hot dog. Within a year, Handwerker rented the ground floor of a building near the corner of Surf and Stillwell Avenues and began selling his own hot dogs for a nickel from behind a twenty-foot (6m)-long counter. By the 1920s, as crowds of people flocked to Coney Island, Nathan's business took off. This marked the beginning of the Nathan's Famous empire, as Handwerker soon sold an average of seventy-five thousand hot dogs every summer weekend. While there is now a chain of Nathan's Famous restaurants, for many people, the only one that matters is the original, found in Coney Island.

Above: This aerial view of Coney Island captures the area's most famous hotel, the Elephant, built by James Lafferty in 1885. It stood 122 feet (37m) high with legs 60 feet (18.5m) in circumference. A spiral staircase in the structure's "hind legs" led up to guest rooms and a gift shop. The hotel's elephant-shaped head provided excellent sea views through the slits of the giant eyes.

CHAPTER ONE

Decadence by the Sea
Coney Island in the Nineteenth Century

Coney Island was nothing more than a desolate five-mile (8km) stretch of sand and scrub when Henry Hudson first laid eyes on it in 1609. Little could he—or anyone—have envisioned that within three centuries, this barren land would become a renowned seaside resort and amusement park that lured thousands to its shores each summer.

Because of Coney Island's ideal location—easily accessible from Manhattan and yet far enough away to provide an escape from the city—it began attracting vacationers in the 1830s and 1840s, as carriage roads and steamship service sliced travel time from as long as half a day to as little as two hours. Grand hotels and inns sprung up on Coney Island's east end to accommodate the growing number of tourists. Beginning in 1829 with the construction of the Coney Island Hotel, development continued with the Brighton, Manhattan Beach, and Oriental Hotels, each one more lavish than the next. Numerous socialites and other notable figures frequented these east end hotels, which created an air of exclusivity and prestige on this part of the peninsula. The hotels offered every amenity available to families vacationing for the summer, including piped-in fresh water, gourmet dinners, security officers who patrolled the beach, and band concerts every evening. Saltwater bathing—a new and novel phenomenon for Americans—slowly gained popularity with the public in the decades after the Civil War, and Coney Island became a primary location for the new "sports" of swimming and sunbathing on the seashore. Each hotel had its own rail line or ferry connection, so patrons could be shuttled directly from Manhattan to their seaside resort, thus largely avoiding the "riffraff" who frequented the rest of the strip.

As the east end was becoming a vacation destination for the well-heeled, the west end, known as Norton Point, developed its own reputation as an area to avoid at all costs. Norton Point was much easier to access from Manhattan, and its convenient location attracted people from all walks of life. Notorious patrons of William Marcy "Boss" Tweed's lawless Tammany Hall political club frequented the area, along with an assortment of underworld figures, vagabonds, gangs, and drunkards. Brawling and verbal altercations were common occurrences—earning the wrath of the hotel guests farther east on the peninsula—and rumors abounded of dead bodies found washed up on the shore.

Into the void between the exclusive east end and the tawdry west end entered John Y. McKane. This shrewd Irish-born constable from Gravesend gained political and economic clout through a series of questionable land deals, and later became the architect of Coney

Island's emerging political machine, especially after the decline of the Tweed ring in 1881. McKane wasted no time developing the center of the strip, known as West Brighton, into a grand commercial venture that he believed would line his wallet with cash while also serving as a monument to his version of modernity.

In 1876, after developer Andrew Culver acquired a three-hundred-foot (91.5m)-tall observation tower—the tallest structure in the United States at the time—from the Philadelphia Centennial Exhibition, McKane succeeded in getting Culver to install it in Coney Island. Bathers could ascend the tower on a steam-powered elevator and then bathe under the udders of a mechanical cow that McKane had installed adjacent to the tower.

Although McKane was given credit for curbing some of the worst of Coney Island's violent crime, he had no interest in making West Brighton anything other than a playground of adult pleasure, and to cash in on each enterprise he helped establish. Despite being an Episcopal Sunday-school teacher who neither smoked nor drank, McKane declared shortly after his election as Coney Island supervisor that "this [was] no Sunday School," and he actively cultivated gambling establishments, giving rise to the rapid proliferation of horse racing as he looked the other way at prostitution and violations of Sunday blue laws.

Below: The Hotel Shelburne was one of the grand hotels that flourished in Coney Island between 1880 and 1920. These spacious hotels frequently had their own restaurants and concert halls.

McKane earned thousands of dollars through the collection of licensing fees from a variety of businesses such as dance and music halls, bathhouses, seedy hotels, shooting galleries, saloons, and even carousels. But, by far, horse racing became the major attraction—its appeal crossed all class barriers. Indeed, Coney Island became America's racetrack capital, bringing with it some of the most

prominent and colorful gamblers of the day—Diamond Jim Brady among them.

By the late 1880s, McKane had gained such enormous power that he had become an important force in county, state, and even federal elections, capable of delivering the thousands of votes belonging to the owners and employees of the enterprises that were beholden to him. However, at the same time, Coney Island's reigning kingmaker was also the target of massive protests by moral reform and temperance crusaders. Preachers and social reformers targeted the gambling and saloon industries as leading causes of crime and debauchery. The Reverend A.C. Dixon's perspective was typical of the wrath expressed by many: "Coney Island, our most popular summer resort, has become a suburb of Sodom. Indeed, Sodom bore no comparison to this place for vileness. One cannot speak in public of the scenes which are daily enacted at that resort and by which young people of both sexes are polluted."

Although McKane increasingly faced charges of consorting with criminals in awarding licenses and of promoting gambling and prostitution, his vast circles of influence allowed him to escape prosecution. Because of the mortgages McKane held on the property of anyone likely to testify against him, there was a dearth of evidence to support a conviction. By 1893, however, McKane had gone one step too far, blatantly rigging an election to prevent a reform candidate from defeating him. Faced with charges of election fraud, contempt of court, misuse of public funds, and nine other crimes, he served four years in Sing Sing, the famous upstate prison. The architect of "Sodom-by-the-Sea," as the *New York Times* called Coney Island, had abruptly fallen from power, never to rise again. A year and a half after McKane's 1898 release from prison, he died of a stroke.

Above: An early lithograph shows the popularity of three-card monte in Coney Island's days of yore. While the difficult-to-reach east end of the strip was an exclusive area set aside for magnificent hotels and restaurants, and the west end was seedy and dangerous, the rest of the area—known as West Brighton—was part of the development scheme of John Y. McKane.

Above: During its peak years, Coney Island offered a variety of concessions. Located conveniently on the same block as food vendors are a hotel, a photo studio, a souvenir shop, a beer hall, and a moving picture pavilion. The Pabst Hotel (left) was a particular favorite of horse racing fans, who came in droves during the late nineteenth and early twentieth centuries. Coney Island's three racetracks were an essential part of the area's early development. Reformers eventually enacted gambling prohibitions in 1910, ending Coney Island's horse racing industry that year.

Paralleling the rise and fall of McKane's empire was the advent of business entrepreneurs who took advantage of Coney Island's rapid growth. Perhaps the most ubiquitous was Charles Feltman. For several years, Feltman had made his living selling fresh-baked pies to the hotels that had begun to proliferate along Coney Island's beaches. When his business patrons began requesting sandwiches to serve their customers, Feltman had to come up with a creative response, given the limited space of his small vending cart. His solution—a small charcoal stove inside the wagon—enabled him to solve the dilemma. Feltman boiled individual pork sausages and then put each one between a roll. He called them "red hots" and then "hot dogs."

Feltman's hot dogs were an immediate hit. The success enabled him to expand his operations, first through the purchase of his own shore lot—at West 10th Street, from Surf Avenue to the beach—and then by opening a series of restaurants and beer gardens. By the 1880s, Feltman had gone from selling 4,000 hot dogs from his pushcart to serving 200,000 patrons in all his establishments. By the first decade of the twentieth century that number had risen to 900,000, and it continued to climb from there. It was only when a former Feltman employee, Nathan Handwerker, created his own establishment in 1916—later to become the legendary Nathan's Famous—that Feltman faced any competition to his hot dog empire in Coney Island.

As the twentieth century beckoned, the area still known as West Brighton drew as many as 300,000 to 500,000 people per day on Saturdays, Sundays, and holidays. At a time when immigrants were flocking to New York en masse from southern and eastern Europe, Coney Island attractions largely attempted to appeal to working-class men and women of limited financial resources, while the east end continued to maintain a wealthy clientele. The main drag on Coney Island—Surf Avenue from Ocean Parkway to West 15th Street—in the 1880s and 1890s was dominated by the Elephant Hotel, which stood 122 feet (37m) high and was built in the shape of an elephant. This landmark hotel, just off of Surf Avenue, faced the ocean and was flanked by an exciting menagerie of amusements, including variety shows, beer saloons, and penny arcades. Perhaps Coney Island's most famous attraction—aside from the hotel itself—was the lane of concessions known as the Bowery, an alley that ran parallel with Surf Avenue. This rough-and-tumble strip—stretching from West 10th to West 16th Street—consisting of shooting galleries, dime museums, slot machines, freak shows, dance halls, and burlesque theaters, was developed by the man who had become the area's most important entrepreneur, the young George Tilyou. In 1882, Tilyou and his father built the Surf Theater, Coney Island's first commercial theater, which stood as the most famous of the Bowery's venues for vaudeville entertainment.

By the 1890s, another important development in West Brighton was the increasing presence of women, especially young women. Concert halls and theaters that attempted to appeal to women and children began to pepper the strip in West Brighton, joining the gambling houses, saloons, and brothels that were male enclaves. Dancing pavilions were especially popular with female patrons, who could find eight such halls at Coney Island, with cultural styles ranging from relatively refined establishments, such as Stauch's Restaurant and Dance Hall, to the seediest saloons, like the Silver Dollar and Perry's Cabaret.

A number of reporters commented on the extraordinary popularity of these pavilions and the dance craze among young women in this era, usually remarking on the differences between "appropriate" and "inappropriate" venues where young women could dance. One account noted: "in the most fashionable [dance hall] there is a good deal of promiscuous intercourse, flirting, and picking up of acquaintances but the dancing itself is usually proper and conventional; in the most Bohemian, behavior is free and pronouncedly bad forms of dancing are seen." In either case, the large crowds found patronizing the dance halls and other amusements on the Bowery and along Surf Avenue reflected a widespread trend in changing male/female social and sexual dynamics. Tilyou understood these dynamics well and would incorporate them into his unique design for the innovation that would define Coney Island and make it world famous as the twentieth century began—the modern amusement park.

Left: Two men, circa 1895, wear the era's unique swimming garb.

Above: During the 1880s and 1890s, the east end of the Coney Island strip, now Brighton Beach and Manhattan Beach, was an exclusive area featuring three luxury hotels: the Brighton Beach, the Manhattan Beach, and the Oriental. In 1885, when this photo was taken, all the beaches on the east end were privately owned by the hotels. As saltwater bathing gained popularity, these hotels thrived and offered their guests gracious accommodations.

Right: This is a pretty risqué shot—given that it was taken in 1898—and is more proof both that the Victorian Era was drawing to a close and that Coney Island's popularity was, in part, about selling sexuality.

Above: Opening day for the Coney Island Bike Path was June 15, 1895. Still in use one hundred years later, the path runs along the median of Ocean Parkway, a magnificent thoroughfare built in the 1870s that led carriages from Prospect Park to the beach.

Above: The first major rail line offering service to Coney Island—beginning with steam engines in 1867—was the Brooklyn, Bath, and Coney Island Railroad. In the late 1870s, August Corbin, railroad magnate and owner of the Manhattan Beach Hotel, built his own rail line, which offered the first direct service to his seaside resort from other points in Brooklyn. The Brighton Beach Hotel followed suit, and direct rail service from Prospect Park through the Brooklyn, Flatbush, and Coney Island Railroad (the Brighton Line) was available as early as 1878. By 1899, the Kings County Elevated Line (which had previously taken over the Brighton Line) was electrified and offered trolley service from Park Row in Manhattan to Coney Island.

Above: Three magnificent and exclusive inns developed on the east end of Coney Island's shore after the Civil War, including the famed Brighton Beach Hotel. Like the Manhattan Beach and Oriental Hotels, the Brighton Beach Hotel was long and wide—measuring 460 by 210 feet (140m by 64m) with room for nearly five thousand people. By 1888, the beach in front of the Brighton Beach Hotel had become so badly eroded that the three-story building, which weighed six thousand tons (5,443t), was moved five hundred feet (152.5m) away from the beach by 120 rail cars.

Below: Manicured lawns graced the fronts of the grand hotels found on Coney Island's east end boardwalk. In the late nineteenth century, this was a summer haven for the well-to-do.

Above: Although it is now hard to imagine not swimming in the ocean on a hot summer's day, saltwater bathing was a relatively new phenomenon in the United States in the late nineteenth century. This picture, dated to the turn of the twentieth century, shows how swimmers used long ropes affixed to the shore to pull themselves in and out of the water lest they be swept away.

Above: When George Tilyou covered his Ferris Wheel with hundreds of lights, the ride immediately became the most popular attraction in Coney Island, setting the stage for the creation of Steeplechase Park. Ferris Wheels soon became a mainstay of many American amusement parks.

CHAPTER TWO

Step Right Up

Steeplechase, Luna Park, Dreamland, and the Evolution of the American Amusement Park

Coney Island had reached extraordinary heights of popularity in the 1890s, but for entreprenuer George Tilyou, the theaters, horse racing, dance halls, and penny arcades were only the beginning. A supreme showman and promoter, Tilyou decided at an early age that if entertainment was what people wanted, he would learn how to give it to them in spades.

Tilyou's inspiration for the grand design of his amusement park began when he visited the Chicago World's Fair during his honeymoon in 1893. Captivated by George Ferris's staggering 250-foot (76m)-in-diameter steel wheel—which held thirty-six cars, each car capable of carrying sixty passengers—Tilyou attempted to buy the Ferris Wheel on the spot. Failing to accomplish this goal, he returned to Coney Island undeterred, ordered a wheel exactly half the size of the one he had seen in Chicago, and placed a sign on the plot of land he had leased on West 8th Street that declared in a most hyperbolic fashion to all who read it: "On this site will be erected the world's largest Ferris Wheel." In no time, Tilyou had rented out enough concession space to pay for the construction of the smaller wheel, and it became Coney Island's most popular attraction of the 1890s.

Tilyou continued to hatch new ideas for rides throughout West Brighton, including the Double-dip Chutes and the Aerial Slide. It was, however, the success of his newest Coney Island competitor, Captain Paul Boyton, that galvanized Tilyou's imagination. Boyton's Sea Lion Park opened in 1895 as the first amusement park where an admission fee was charged upon entrance. The park was enclosed by a fence and featured rides and concessions clustered together inside. Boyton—a long-distance swimmer who had made a name for himself by paddling for miles in a rubber suit designed for use as a new life-saving device—bought land behind the Elephant Hotel for the amusement park. Here he developed his signature ride, named Shoot the Chutes, in which passengers sat in flat-bottomed boats that slid dramatically down a long, steep slide into a lagoon.

The popularity of Sea Lion Park was all that Tilyou needed to develop his own amusement park empire, which would soon leave Boyton and his chutes in the dust. Taking his inspiration from the enormous popularity of horse racing, Tilyou brought the British steeplechase ride to Coney Island, giving it a beachfront home in an amusement park that stretched from West 16th to West 19th Streets. Passengers "raced" each other while riding on wooden horses that ran on wheels around a narrow curving metal track that included steep inclines, hills, and hurdles. In 1897, Steeplechase Park opened its doors to the public.

Tilyou understood early on that the dynamics of successful entertainment entailed more than the rides and attractions themselves. He wanted his customers to interact with each other, to make themselves part of the show. He also liked to surprise and titillate his patrons by knocking them off balance, blowing their hats off, or, in the case of rides such as the Wedding Ring and the Barrel of Love, rocking them back and forth so that men and women—including many who had boarded the rides as strangers—often had no choice but to tumble into or hang on to one another. In fact, patrons entering the park through the main boardwalk entrance had to pass through the Barrel of Love, a slowly revolving fifteen-foot (4.5m)-long cylinder of wood. Tilyou's Dew Drop, a parachute ride down a fifty-foot (15m)-tall tower, became well-known for lifting women's skirts for the pleasure of any and all voyeurs. Like the Barrel of Love, attractions such as the Earthquake Float, the Dancing Floor, and the Human Roulette Wheel all capitalized on the notion that young men and women liked any excuse to grab hold of and touch each other.

Tilyou knew who his customers were and kept his prices affordable for working people, many of whom saved their hard-earned money all summer just to spend it at Steeplechase Park. He added other attractions in 1905, such as a miniature steam railroad, a large saltwater swimming pool, and the largest ballroom in New York state, which featured four brass bands. He also constructed a pedestrian arcade that ran from Surf Avenue to Steeplechase Pier, enabling electric cars to bring ferry passengers directly into his park.

What was perhaps Tilyou's most ambitious new attraction was unveiled in 1902, a science-fiction-themed ride called A Trip to the Moon. It was operated by Frederic Thompson, a draftsman and designer who attempted to use the latest technologies in lighting, sound, and motion to create a fantasy of space travel. On their way to the imaginary voyage to the moon, passengers experienced electrical storms, bolts of lightning, and the sounds of howling wind.

Steeplechase's personality could be well summed up by the toothy, deviously jesterlike character featured on the park's logo. It suggested that customers might be a bit surprised and even frightened by what they found as they walked through the gates of the amusement park, but they would be endlessly entertained at what Tilyou referred to as "The Funny Place." His attempts to make the audience the unwitting dupes of their own vaudeville shows were best reflected through attractions like the Human Zoo, in which patrons climbed a spiral staircase and found themselves unknowingly thrust into a cage with monkeys, or his most P.T. Barnum–like practical joke, the California Red Bats, in which he seduced a gullible audience into climbing a steep flight of steps to search for a secret treasure that was nothing more than a box containing broken bricks.

It appeared as though Tilyou's staggering success could go on end-lessly, but in July of 1907 a fire broke out in the Cave of the Winds attraction. Although only a few people were seriously injured in the fire that burned for eighteen hours, most of Steeplechase Park was destroyed. Without missing a beat, Tilyou, on the very next day, erected a sign where the entrance had been that read, "To inquiring friends: I had troubles yesterday that I have not had today. On this site will be erected shortly a bigger, better Steeplechase Park. Admission to the Burning Ruins: 10 cents." And true to his word, in nine months, Steeplechase and Tilyou were back in business. But this time he had serious competition for Coney Island's amusement dollar from two other competitors.

Frederic Thompson, the architect behind the futuristic ride A Trip to the Moon, had his own ideas about creating an amusement park—and he put them to work in 1903 when he designed Luna Park at Surf Avenue between West 8th and West 12th Streets. Thompson and his partner, Elmer "Skip" Dundy, wanted the audience to be transported to a fairy-tale world of space travel and underwater adventure, jungles and deserts, safaris and battles. In designing the park, Thompson made a point of eliminating all straight lines and conventional forms, making Luna Park look and feel like an ancient

Above: A signature ride of Steeplechase Park, The Barrel of Love was a revolving tunnel that threw strangers into one another. In ways both subtle and direct, Tilyou created environments that allowed young men and women to physically interact with one another. In his ad for this ride, Tilyou declared, "Talk about love in a cottage! This has it beat by a mile."

Far Eastern temple. For the park's extraordinary opening night spectacle, they decorated the forest of high arching towers and steeples with a quarter of a million incandescent lights, dazzling viewers who had never seen anything remotely like it in their lives. Indeed, Luna Park felt bigger than life—just what Thompson and Dundy had in mind.

While Tilyou favored raucous gags and vaudeville tomfoolery, Thompson and Dundy found their inspiration in awe-inspiring sensation, extravagance, and excess, creating huge thrill rides that attempted to simulate people's most extreme fantasies about the new modern era that lay ahead. From the War of the Worlds Building, where the audience defended New York Harbor against small-scale versions of the navies of European powers, to the Twenty Thousand Leagues Under the Sea submarine ride, where passengers observed an authentically rendered North Pole with real seals and polar bears, Luna Park fed the early-twentieth-century frenzy for disaster spectacles, science fiction, and "you are there" adventure journeys. Thompson and Dundy also believed that people desired constant change, and they added new rides each year, including crowd pleasers such as the Tickler and the Mountain Torrent.

Luna Park also specialized in providing its own versions of "exotic" foreign cultures to its patrons—including German, Irish, and Eskimo villages, a Chinese theater, a Delhi marketplace, and the canals of Venice—creating an alternate universe for people who might never travel beyond America's borders or even cross New York's state line. The newspapers described the Delhi procession as so magnificent "as to make those who witnessed it imagine they were in a genuine Oriental City." The reproduction included gilded chariots, prancing horses, trained elephants, and dancing girls.

"Authentic" reenactments were one of Thompson and Dundy's specialties, and the public responded with unbridled enthusiasm. The pair's efforts to simulate the Russian-Japanese war using forty miniature battleships sailing around a harbor while the two opposing armies bombarded each other stood as a typical example of Luna Park's ability to appeal to Americans' pre–World War I fascination with conflict and conquest.

Perhaps the most unique of Luna Park's exhibits was Dr. Courtney's Infant Incubator. Thousands of people, mostly women, entrusted a stranger with their prematurely born babies in the belief that the doctor could save the children with a technique so new and radical that hospitals wouldn't allow him to practice it. Thompson and Dundy, however, were glad to welcome Dr. Courtney to Luna Park, and Courtney saved the vast majority of babies brought to him.

The success of both Luna Park and Steeplechase in the first decade of the new century stood as a signal to many observers that Coney Island could easily accommodate another amusement park. State Senator William Reynolds, best known for his shady real estate dealings, would be the one who would attempt to create a grand amusement park even bigger and better than its predecessors.

Reynolds wanted his Dreamland to symbolize the future on every level, to showcase the newest and most sensational modern technology, and to outflank Luna Park for sheer size and spectacle. If Luna Park had a quarter of a million electric lights, Dreamland would have one million. If Luna Park firefighters fought imaginary flames in a building four feet (1m) high, then Dreamland's building would be two feet (0.5m) higher. Reynold's location along the seashore, adjacent to Steeplechase, would ensure that his master-piece would outdo all others.

Dreamland cost more than two million dollars to build, more than three times as much as Luna Park, quite a staggering figure in 1904 when the newer park was completed. It was large enough to fit a hundred thousand people comfortably and had the grandest dance hall in the entire state of New York. Dreamland's steel pier stretched out to sea for nearly half a mile (0.8km) and, because it was built around an actual inlet of the ocean, visitors could arrive by steam-boat from a variety of terminals in Manhattan.

Although Dreamland competed for Luna Park's tony audience through grander and larger-scale scenarios of exotic cultural and cur-rent event reenactments, the newer park may have differentiated itself most dramatically through its psychological morality plays. At a time when Coney Island was condemned by many middle-class

Above: In 1910, Coney Island's Bowery—the strip that ran six blocks from Steeplechase Park to Feltman's restaurant—was flooded with people and plenty of opportunities to eat, drink, and be merry.

reformers for promoting unbridled hedonism and rampant sexuality, Reynolds and the park's creative director, George Dobson, developed attractions such as Creation and The End of the World, which attempted to teach their audience lessons of virtue and chastity. If Dreamland represented the future, it was a future that took its ethical cues from the Bible rather than from the popular culture of the era.

The End of the World frightened its viewers by depicting sinners who sank into a red pit while the angel Gabriel blew the trumpet of doom. Creation, the first amusement that visitors passed as they entered the park, transported its riders to the birth of the universe with Adam and Eve in the Garden of Eden. Both of these heavy-handed biblically themed attractions used scenes of hell and images of Satan as analogies for the then–modern day terrors that might befall audience members, especially young women. The fate of those women who veered from the straight and narrow path and chose "loose" morals instead of marital monogamy, or the saloon rather than the church, looked very bleak according to these spectacles. Even Dreamland's "white city" imagery and its attempt to create architectural symmetry in its outward appearance had almost religious overtones, leaving its visitors with a clear delineation between the "good" found within Dreamland's gates and the "evil" found in the Bowery's dancehalls.

Although people initially flocked to Dreamland, its popularity soon declined. Reynold's dream never sustained the crowds enjoyed by Steeplechase or Luna Park, despite luring six concessions away from the latter, including Dr. Courtney's famed Infant Incubator. Despite the architectural splendor and aspirations to higher cultural values, many observers believed that the newer park's owners didn't fully understand popular taste. Even though people continued to attend its technology exhibits, Dreamland's numbers began to increase again only after the park added freak shows such as the Congress of Curious People and the Lilliputian Village.

For the 1911 season, Dreamland's owners invested an additional sixty thousand dollars to upgrade and renovate their park in the hope of boosting attendance. The white city was no more, replaced by a repainted cream-and-bright-red color scheme. Things looked promising as Memorial Day weekend, symbolizing the beginning of summer, arrived, and with Sam Gumpertz installed as Dreamland's new manager. Late on the night of May 27, as workers were furiously trying to fix a leak inside the Hell Gate Boat Ride, the circuitry began to malfunction, the lights went out, and one of the men accidentally knocked over a bucket of hot tar, starting a fire that eventually engulfed the entire park. By the next day, there was nothing left of Dreamland but smoldering ashes. Reynolds suffered a three-million-dollar loss but was able to make back some of his investment by selling the property to the city. Nevertheless, he and his partners decided not to rebuild, and the grand vision of Dreamland was forever relegated to the colorful history of Coney Island.

Above: Dreamland, always trying to outdo its rival Luna Park, created a larger version of Shooting the Chutes, calling their version Shoot the Chutes. The two chutes built side by side created the largest water slide ever. It had a 280-foot (85.5m) ramp plus a 360-foot (110m) escalator that took passengers to the top of the slide before they descended into the lagoon below.

Right: This is the ride that made Steeplechase famous and from which it took its name. When Tilyou rebuilt his park in 1908, he created this larger and improved Steeplechase ride. The eight horses, seating two riders each, raced around the rails. During the course of their rides, passengers plunged across a small body of water, up hills to a height of sixteen feet (5m) above the beach, and back down and through a tunnel before they navigated a series of hurdles on their way to the finish line.

Above: The remains of the first Steeplechase Park are surveyed after the 1907 fire destroyed many of the amusements. Note that Tilyou's signature logo, with its slightly devious smile, still remains front and center. The day after the fire, Tilyou erected a sign announcing that he would build a new "bigger and better Steeplechase Park."

Above: Tilyou was not kidding when he told his public that the new Steeplechase would be bigger and better than the first. When the park reopened in 1908, it included eight roller coasters, a large ballroom for dancing, the raucous Pavilion of Fun, an enormous swimming pool, and a longer and much-improved Steeplechase ride.

Above: A visit to the new-and-improved Steeplechase would not be complete without a stop in The Pavilion of Fun, which featured the infamous Blowhole Theater (pictured), the Insanitarium, Comedy Lane, Battleship Roll, the Laughing Gallery, the Human Pool Table, and many other amusements. The Blowhole was notorious for its system of compressed air jets that sent women's dresses and skirts swirling in the breeze for all to look beneath. Given that America was only recently leaving behind the repressive Victorian Era, these types of entertainments can be seen as emblematic of a significant shift in social mores.

Above: When Tilyou reopened his park in 1908, he built the largest outdoor swimming pool in the country. The pool measured 270 by 90 feet (82.5m by 27.5m) and contained 670,000 gallons (2,535,950L) of salt water.

Below: From this angle it's easy to get a sense of the enormity of the Steeplechase swimming pool. There was a special bathing section for children, who were becoming a significant part of the park's clientele. In addition, the area surrounding the big outdoor pool featured bathing beauty contests each summer—another big draw for participants and voyeurs alike.

Right: Amusement parks provided a popular destination for families. Steeplechase Park, in particular, offered many special rides and attractions for children, although the evening ambience was decidedly adult.

Left: Frederic Thompson's architectural background influenced the design that he and his partner, Skip Dundy, created for Luna Park, which was peppered with tall towers—more than one thousand by the time they were finished.

Above: Beyond the great entrance to Luna Park stood a broad avenue called the Court of Honor, which was bordered on one side by Luna's signature attraction, A Trip to the Moon, on the other by a recreated Venetian city equipped with a Grand Canal and an illuminated bridge with gondoliers.

Above: At night, Luna Park's quarter of a million incandescent lights filled the sky and created an extraordinary feast for the eyes.

Above: Luna Park's Mountain Torrent ride, opened in 1906, combined features from both roller coasters and waterslides. Customers lumbered up to an 80-foot (24.5m)-high peak, where they boarded cars that raced down a water flume on a track. The ride culminated dramatically with a splash in a lake at the bottom.

Above: Shooting the Chutes was one of Luna Park's most popular attractions. This image shows passengers at the very end of the ride as they glide into the artificial lake.

Above: Luna Park specialized in bringing cultural spectacles to the streets of Coney Island. Pictured here is an ornately decorated float celebrating the park's first Mardi Gras, circa 1915.

Above: In this picture, Luna Park looks particularly posh as people promenade along its walkways. Note the proper dress for leisurely activity along the beach—today, one would never see this level of formality in an amusement park.

Left: From the Tickler's opening in 1907, it remained among Luna Park's most popular rides. It seemed people truly enjoyed bouncing through a maze on a constantly curving path as they rode in giant saucerlike cups mounted on coaster wheels that twirled and whirled down inclined slopes.

Above: There were several versions of the Whip, a ride that rapidly whirled passengers sitting in small cars. The one pictured here premiered at Luna Park around 1910. There were also independent versions of the same ride that appeared both on the Bowery and on Surf Avenue.

Below: After Dundy's death, Thompson's financial problems multiplied and he lost Luna Park to creditors in 1912. In 1917, Luna's new general manager, Oscar Jurney, added a new attraction, located beside the Whip, called the Top (aka the Scenic Spiral Wheel), to the park's amusements. Bound by the laws of gravity and centrifugal force, the Top was a forty-five ton (41t) steel wheel that slowly rotated on its side.

Above: Both Luna Park and Dreamland attempted to simulate adventure through rides that sought to transport the passenger to another time and place. This landscape in Luna Park reflects a desire to create a Western milieu, and appears to be part of the Grand Canyon Toboggan Railway.

Above: War reenactments were an extremely popular feature in Luna Park. Inspired by the Battle of Château-Thierry, an American and French offensive launched against the Germans during World War I, the Luna Park version used electric flashes, drums, rifles, and machine guns to create the "real" feeling of battle.

Left: Elephant rides were another Luna Park specialty—this attraction was so heavily promoted that, on one occasion, the park brought in silent-movie idol Douglas Fairbanks to show it off. These types of publicity stunts worked so well that, together, the two elephants Thompson and Dundy purchased in 1909 carried nearly ten thousand people per week on their backs.

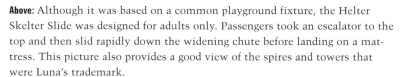

Above: Although it was based on a common playground fixture, the Helter Skelter Slide was designed for adults only. Passengers took an escalator to the top and then slid rapidly down the widening chute before landing on a mattress. This picture also provides a good view of the spires and towers that were Luna's trademark.

Above: The Helter Skelter Slide provided thrills for onlookers as well as its passengers. Skirts were prone to flying up in the air as women rollicked down the giant slide.

Right: Dreamland's towering spheres were stunning. Seeing them at night for the first time, author and poet Albert Bigelow Paine commented: "Tall towers that had grown dim suddenly broke forth in electric outlines and gay rosettes of color, as the living sparks of light travel hither and thither until the place was transformed into an electric garden, of such a sort as Aladdin never dreamed." To guarantee that the towers were the first things that visitors arriving by steamship would see, Dreamland had its own pier.

Above: At the dawn of the twentieth century, disaster reenactments had become a morbid source of public fascination. Coney Island entrepreneurs were quick to capitalize on this curiosity by creating a number of exhibitions such as the Johnstown Flood—an exhibition depicting the 1889 flood in Johnstown, Pennsylvania, which killed more than two thousand people. Other similar disaster reenactments included the Burning of Natchez, the Volcanic Eruption of Mount Pelée, and the San Francisco Earthquake of 1906. These amusements were typically far more likely to be found at Dreamland or Luna Park than they were at Steeplechase.

Above: Awesome in its stature, with grand architectural pretensions and a bright white facade, Dreamland offered fantasy adventures and dramatic simulations. As an example of the latter, spectators of Fighting the Flames watched a cast of 120 firefighters with four fire trucks act out the rescue of several hundred actors from a six-story hotel engulfed in flames. Ironically, Dreamland was the victim of an accidental fire that destroyed the entire park in 1911.

Left: In addition to disaster reenactments, another popular Coney Island attraction during the early twentieth century was the "mini village"—usually an attempt to depict culture and traditions that amusement park creators undoubtedly considered exotic, typically those of Africa, Asia, or the South Pacific. This image is from the Borneo Village at Dreamland, and shows the making of a war shield.

Above: Another image from the Borneo Village at Dreamland shows a man constructing a pipe out of wood. While these "mini villages" certainly reflected a belief that these cultures were "primitive" and even "savage," based on Western notions of racial superiority, they also reflected curiosity about the world outside American borders. Samuel Gumpertz, Dreamland's manager, in an attempt at authenticity, supposedly went as far as to "acquire" nineteen "wild men" from Borneo from a tribal leader in exchange for two hundred bags of salt.

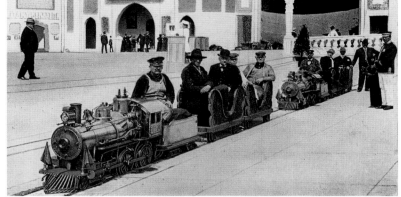

Left: The Miniature Railroad could be found at the center of Dreamland. Built by the Cagney Brothers, who were pioneers of amusement park trains, these trains had two small cars, each of which held two passengers, and were pulled by tiny steam locomotives.

Above: Not much of Dreamland's splendor is recognizable in its remains after the fire in 1911. Ironically, the fire started at an attraction called the Hell Gate. Within a few hours, the flames were raging uncontrollably throughout the entire park. Given the amount of money its owners had originally invested in Dreamland, rebuilding it after the fire was deemed too difficult and costly.

Above: Aside from Steeplechase, Luna Park, and Dreamland, independent rides sprang up all over Coney Island to capitalize on the overflowing traffic from the large amusement parks. The Tunnels of Love was a staple of the Coney Island experience, selling notions of romance and sexual titillation via a slow-moving boat ride through dimly lit tunnels. This ride attracted both men and women, and young people in particular.

Above: Coney Island had its share of frauds and swindles. Perhaps the biggest was Samuel Friede's Globe Tower—a space-age plan for the largest theme park in the world, all in a sphere topping a seven-hundred-foot (213.5m) tower. The grand design for the Globe included restaurants, hotels, theaters, a roller skating rink, and a bowling alley. There were also plans for an observation deck at the very top, while the bottom of the structure would boast a parking garage, subway, and railroad station. Friede was able to con a number of investors into funding his grandiose scheme. However, when no further work was completed on the tower after Friede orchestrated two cornerstone-laying ceremonies in 1906 and again in 1907, it became clear that the project was a fraud.

Above: Although fast rides became the rage of the amusement park scene, there were still many opportunities for slower paced attractions such as this one, where a swan-shaped car pulls riders through scenic surroundings.

Above: Coney Island amusement parks featured an enormous variety of activities: carnivals, mini international villages, arcade games, and freak shows. Circus performers took their cue from P.T. Barnum's big top and featured acrobats, high-wire acts, and lion tamers, as well as sideshow characters.

Above: This view of Surf Avenue's main drag during the roaring 1920s highlights Coney Island's development from a recreational seaside community into a thriving commercial and business sector—and a growing residential neighborhood.

Entertaining the Masses
Coney Island in the 1920s and 1930s

Even with Dreamland's demise, Coney Island continued to attract ever larger numbers of people, especially after the extension of the subway to Brooklyn from Manhattan in 1920 made travel both easier and cheaper than before. Increasingly, masses of working-class men and women on day trips comprised the bulk of these visitors and, thus, the remaining fashionable resorts on the east end of the strip declined. The number of grand hotels dwindled even further when two of the grandest hotels, the Manhattan Beach and the Oriental, closed prior to World War I.

Not surprisingly, Steeplechase Park was best equipped to respond to the demands of the majority of Coney Island consumers, and owner George Tilyou scored big with his new Blowhole Theater, colorful carousels, and an enormous swimming pool, which he claimed was the world's largest. Even after Tilyou's sudden death in 1914, his son Edward carried on without a hitch—at least until the onset of the Great Depression.

Luna Park continued to attract a stout following, but after 1920 it began a steady decline in popularity due in large part to a diminishing public interest in disasters and battles as the world attempted to recover from the Great War in Europe. Reality-based theater was out of fashion. Fun-house attractions, elaborate skill games, and fast rides—especially roller coasters—were in.

As the automobile took on the role of status symbol and amateur aviation gained a cultlike following, the American public of the roaring 1920s relished speed and excitement. Although roller coasters had existed since the 1880s, it was the new modern machines built during the 1920s that captured the popular imagination. As the technology advanced, rides were constructed to travel higher and faster, exactly what their thrill-seeking passengers desired. Some of the most famous roller coasters of this era included the Thunderbolt, built in 1925, the 1926 Tornado, and the legendary and still-functioning Cyclone, built in 1927. These new coasters gained such extraordinary popularity that, during some summer weekends, people waited in lines for up to five hours for these exhilarating and sometimes terrifying rides that lasted for just a few minutes. Although serious accidents did occur, these newer roller coasters were generally safer than their predecessors and problems with the rides were few and far between. Far more frequent were the skirmishes and fights that erupted when tempers flared on torrid summer nights among the huge crowds of people impatient for their turn on these new modern marvels.

The extension of the subway brought millions of lower-income New Yorkers to Coney Island and served as the impetus for opening up the beach and constructing breakwaters and jetties for its preservation. Prior to 1923, virtually all the shoreline was privately owned and visitors had to pay both to use the beach and to change in private bathhouses. In addition to making the entire beach public, new sand was added to create extra beachfront space to accommodate more people. The seashore became a destination of choice, and crowds of people packed Coney Island's beaches on stifling summer weekends. Public bathhouses, where lockers could be rented for twenty-five cents each, were built and, in 1921, Mayor John Francis Hyland formally opened the boardwalk to the public, bringing a proliferation of new pushcarts and hot dog stands. Picnics on the beach emerged as a popular family pastime.

Coney Island acquired a nickname, the "Empire of the Nickel," because that was all the money it took for people to partake in numerous delights at the playground on the Atlantic. In the 1930s, the Works Progress Administration's guide to New York described the scene this way: "From early morning when the first throngs pour from the Stillwell Avenue subway terminal, humanity flows over Coney seeking relief from the heat of the city. Italians, Jews, Greeks, Poles, Germans, Negroes, Irish, people of every nationality push and collide as they rush, laughing, scolding, sweating, for a spot on the sand."

The reference here to "Negroes" in the description of the cultural mix represented on a typical Coney Island beach day does not mention that, although African-Americans did begin to come to Coney Island en masse as their numbers increased in New York City in the 1920s and 1930s, they often continued to face de facto segregation on the beach and in the amusement parks. The same can be said of the music halls and dance pavilions that frequently hired black entertainers but rarely tolerated racial mixing among the clientele. The years leading up to World War II included some blatantly racist carnival sideshows, including one in which black men were exploited as targets for customers throwing softballs.

By the 1920s and into the 1930s, attendance on a summer Sunday could climb to more than a million people, more than 18 percent of the entire population of New York City. From the boardwalk, one could look far and wide and not see an empty patch of sand. Given that only forty years earlier the idea of bathing in an ocean seemed so strange and foreign to the first tourists to Coney Island that they sought advice from a doctor regarding what they should wear, the transformation was rapid and complete.

After the racetracks folded in 1910, leading to a decline in gambling and prostitution, moral reformers focused their attention on public indecency on the beach, especially topless male bathing, an increasingly popular practice as Coney Island's numbers grew. The traditional male bathing suits of the day covered the entire torso, were slow to dry, and tended to become unbearably itchy when infiltrated

Left: The completion of the subway from Manhattan to Brooklyn's Stillwell Avenue in 1919 dramatically increased the number of people who came to Coney Island. In the next few years, their destination became known as the "Nickel Empire" because ordinary citizens—including the working class and poor—were now able to reach Coney Island's beach and amusement parks for only a five-cent subway ride. This kind of scene, with crowded lines of people waiting for the "longest and safest ride on Coney Island," presumably on the train, became typical during this era.

by even the smallest amounts of sand. Until Mayor Fiorello La Guardia came out in favor of bare-chested swimming for men in the late 1930s, however, the exposure of men's nipples could and did result in fines and sometimes arrests. Similar controversies concerning women's bathing suits would come considerably later.

After dark, Coney Island's nightlife took over on the Bowery—its music halls jammed for vaudevillians such as Eddie Cantor and Jimmy Durante, who took center stage at Carey Walsh's cabaret, while Vincent Lopez played piano in a five-person orchestra at Perry's Glass Pavilion. With the advent of Prohibition, many of the saloons became speakeasies that hired bouncers to maintain order. These men were a notorious lot that for a short time included legendary gangster Al Capone. The Bowery was the midway, the center for Coney Island's carnival life, with penny arcades, waxwork museums, freak shows, fortunetellers, and funhouses. Future Hollywood movie star Cary Grant began his career as an acrobat in Coney Island. Hired by George Tilyou's son to walk on stilts through the Bowery, Grant was a part of Steeplechase Park's advertising campaign.

Broadway producers of the 1920s and 1930s such as Moss Hart and George S. Kaufman also found Coney Island's theaters to be good venues for previewing their plays and musicals. Hart and Kaufman's *Once in a Lifetime* premiered at Coney prior to beginning its extended run on Broadway. Jazz, ragtime, and Viennese waltzes could all be found among the various Bowery venues.

Although Coney Island's recreations continued to attract large crowds throughout the 1930s, the Great Depression had a significant impact on many of the area's proprietors. The American economy was devastated and Coney Island's Bowery was no exception. Charles

Right: After Luna Park's Virginia Reel closed, this independent version of the ride opened on the Bowery in 1924. The popular ride featured rotating circular cars that spun around a serpentine track down an incline, eventually coming to an end in a whirlpool. Adjacent to the Virginia Reel is Coney Island's most famous Ferris Wheel, the Wonder Wheel. Over 130 feet (39.5m) tall, and capable of carrying 150 people dispersed in a total of twenty-four cars, the Wonder Wheel was built on the boardwalk in 1920 and is still in use today.

Feltman, who had parlayed his hot dog empire into a successful restaurant, saw his business steadily decline throughout the decade as cheap food sold from pushcarts was all many visitors to Coney Island could afford in addition to their round-trip subway fare. Likewise, the decline in the average New Yorker's disposable income contributed to the failure of vaudeville acts, which were already being decimated by the popularity of the motion picture industry.

Amusement parks continued to report large attendance numbers, but people spent less money overall, and Luna Park in particular suffered financially from a continuing lack of adequate capital. Prior to a declaration of bankruptcy in 1933, Luna Park's owners attempted to cut costs by toning down the spectacles—eliminating the more costly animal amusements and even substituting pigs for elephants in one instance, and giving out crackers and sugar as prizes for games rather than Kewpie dolls. They also reduced the adult admission to ten cents on weekdays and twenty cents on weekends, but attendance continued to decrease. During some seasons, Luna Park lit only a fraction of its lights—once the cornerstone of its very existence—and failed to repaint its rides. Various new owners attempted to revive the park but failed to appreciably increase attendance and revenue. In August 1944, after a fire at the Dragon Gorge Scenic Railroad destroyed half of the park and led to damages of as much as half a million dollars, Luna quietly completed its summer season and closed forever.

The Depression also paralleled Robert Moses's tenure as the New York City Parks Commissioner and head of the Triborough Bridge and Tunnel Authority. In 1938, the powerful parks commissioner persuaded Mayor La Guardia to allow him to take over regulation of the beach and the boardwalk. Moses, known for his obsession with orderliness, began to rein in what he viewed as the excessive noise and commotion created by the carnival barkers and sideshow promoters. He issued a maze of violations that effectively put most of the touts and their shows out of business. The commissioner also established a series of prohibitions for the bathing area and boardwalk in an attempt to clean up Coney Island's anarchic beach culture. Although some reformers praised Moses for creating regulations necessary to preserve the civility and cleanliness of the shorefront, others believed that his heavy-handed rules reflected an overall disdain for Coney Island's raffish legacy. Either way, the years leading up to America's entry into World War II represented an end to the Nickel Empire and Coney Island's ascendance. The postwar years would usher in a new and uncertain era.

Left: Beauty pageants thrived in Coney Island in the 1920s. Here we see the Misses Coney Island of 1924 and 1925 photographed together.

Above: Not everyone who came to Coney Island during its Nickel Empire days arrived by subway. As this parking lot shows, many beach-bound travelers chose to make the trip by private car, especially after Robert Moses created the first parkways to go through Brooklyn and into eastern Long Island.

Above: Although the first roller coasters were erected in the 1880s, and many more flourished in Coney Island, the Cyclone—built for $100,000 in 1927— was the largest of its kind and featured an eighty-six-foot (26m) drop. When it first opened, lines stretched for blocks. The Cyclone continues to run, pleasing the public more than seventy-five years after its opening on Surf Avenue.

Above: Bob's Coaster Baths, along with sundry other establishments, were nestled at the foot of the Tornado, one of Coney's three great roller coasters. Erected on the Bowery in 1926, this bobsledlike ride was destroyed by fire in 1977.

Above: The Municipal Bath was the largest of Coney Island's bathhouses, with twelve thousand lockers available to day-trippers. Prior to the 1920s, bathhouses in the area were all privately owned and visitors had to pay large fees to use them. By contrast, the Municipal Bath was affordable and open to the public. As reflected in this photo, people wanting to use the beach gathered in long lines and waited for hours to snare a locker. Later, during the Depression, the practice of wearing a bathing suit under one's clothes to save time and money became more common.

Above: Here's a side view of the Thunderbolt from Steeplechase's pool area. Built in 1925, this wooden and steel structure was designed by renowned roller coaster engineer John Miller and continued running until 1983.

Above: Although there was little attention paid to children in the early designs for Coney Island, by the 1920s and 1930s, a family outing to Coney had become a favorite and scenes like this one were commonplace.

Below: The entire seashore at Coney Island became public in 1923, but ropes and posts were still used to divide different areas of the beach, as well as to aid bathers in moving in and out of the water.

Left: A good example of contrasting colors at the seashore shows that, whether you chose white or black swimwear, bare-chested bathing was out of the realm of the permissible for anyone, children included, until after the 1930s.

Above: This aerial photograph from the 1930s shows far more people on the boardwalk than on the beach on a Sunday afternoon. Note that the long steel pier used by the amusement parks to bring passengers to shore from steamboats remains a presence on the beach, despite the growing prevalence of rail travel.

Below: Beauty pageants were well-attended events at the Coney Island amusement parks, bringing in both male and female audiences and selling a certain brand of sexuality that became connected to summer beach culture.

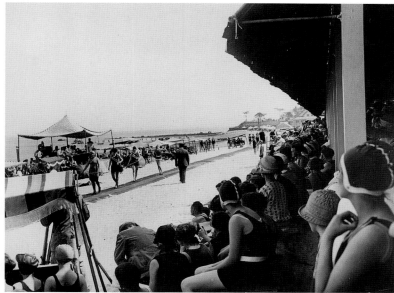

Right: Men pack a penny arcade in this picture from the 1930s. During the Depression, skee-ball, a carnival adaptation of bowling, gained tremendous popularity. Note here the signs encouraging both men and women to patronize the establishment, though, in this photo, all the game players appear to be male.

Below: Well before making his mark as "Mr. Television" in the 1950s, comedian Milton Berle (left) is shown here, with dance troupe leader George Hale, measuring some aspect of the physical dimensions of eighteen-year-old Grayce Reilly, after she had won the twenty-sixth Modern Venus Bathing Beauty Contest at Steeplechase Park in 1939.

Above: Trapeze and high-wire acts became commonplace, especially during the peak years of the Nickel Empire, when millions of people crowded the amusement parks on summer weekends.

Left: A man plays Ring the Bell, while two others look on. The electric tattoo parlor in the background was likely a popular attraction on Coney Island's Bowery. So was the Tattooed Lady who, with seven hundred designs and pictures inscribed in her skin, appeared in amusement park sideshows.

Above: In addition to rides, parades, and miniature villages, arcade games were favorites at Coney Island amusement parks. In this photo, Luna Park customers are lined up for Chute the Pig, a game in the 1920s that featured a piglet sliding down a chute when participants accurately pitched a small ball at a target.

Above: This 1922 photograph shows three well-heeled women representing the "Society Circus Committee" for a Manhattan street fair. The ladies hold five Luna Park piglets, and presumably await instructions on how to run their circus.

Right: Luna Park's founders, Fred Thompson and Skip Dundy, loved to use live animals, elephants in particular, for their rides and amusements. Dundy regarded elephants as good luck charms and claimed to have the largest show herd in the world. Although Dundy died in 1907 and Thompson in 1919, this image from the 1920s shows that their influence long outlived them. Here, a string of scantily clad women pose with one of the park's elephant calves and its trainer.

Opposite: Large crowds frequented the Bowery in Coney Island, a midway of amusement concessions, dance halls, dime museums, and penny arcades. The Red Devil Rider was an independently owned roller coaster that operated between 1907 and the late 1920s.

Above: Sideshow circus freaks were a big part of Coney Island culture—first at Dreamland and later in the other two parks—as entrepreneurs continued the P.T. Barnum tradition. Even in the decades before the emergence of a movement for disabled-citizen rights, these shows had critics for the vulgar manner in which they exploited people with extreme physical deformities. At the same time, some believed that these sideshows provided a sense of community and consistent employment for people who might otherwise have been ostracized.

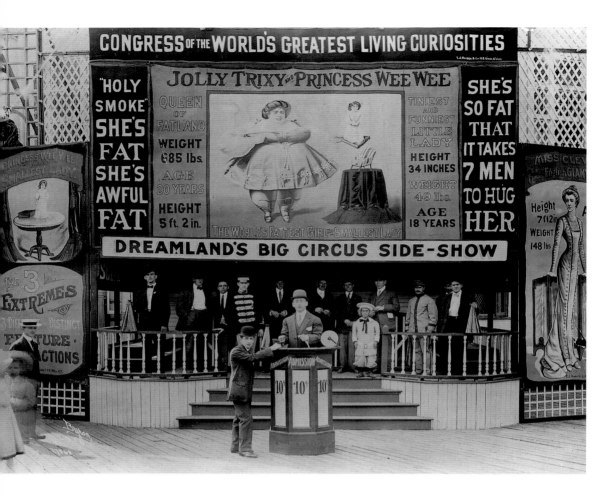

Above: Dreamland's Fat Lady attraction was a particular favorite of manager Samuel Gumpertz. This image shows the manner in which he promoted one woman, Jolly Trixy. Note that seven-hundred-pound (317kg) Trixy is juxtaposed with her physical opposite, Princess WeeWee who, at eighteen years of age, measured less than three feet tall (0.9m) and weighed forty-nine pounds (22kg).

Above: Here's a typical scene from the sidelines of a Coney Island freak show: two performers, an albino and a fat lady, discuss business with two other unidentified individuals. Note the flea circus posters in the background.

Above: Carnival barkers were a favorite with the crowds, but not with Robert Moses. Upon becoming parks commissioner, he created numerous ordinances designed to curtail what he viewed as a cacophonous disturbance to Coney Island's decorum. Without the ability to draw potential customers inside, freak shows suffered hard times even after the Depression.

Above: A young man eats corn on the cob from a food stand along the boardwalk. During the Depression, cheap food that could be eaten while walking increasingly replaced many of the sit-down establishments.

Above: During the Great Depression of the 1930s, when people had little disposable income, Coney Island's inexpensive food stands along the boardwalk and the Bowery were enormously popular. Here, patrons buy hot corn and hamburgers for a nickel each, the same price as a subway token.

Right: Fires devastated Coney Island on several occasions—destroying the first Steeplechase Park in 1907 and then Dreamland in 1911. The biggest fire, however, occurred not in an amusement park but in a residential area (shown) in June 1932, when four boys decided to burn rubbish they found under the boardwalk at West 22nd Street. The tinder-dry rubbish and a strong wind blowing off the water resulted in the flames spreading to several concession stands before the first fire company could arrive. The flames continued at will and spread from West 21st to West 24th Street along the boardwalk and to Surf Avenue.

Below: A total of 178 buildings were destroyed in the 1932 blaze, which left more than one thousand people homeless and caused more than five million dollars in property damage. After this fire, $400,000 would be used to purchase a new high-pressure water system. Nevertheless, a 1944 fire subsequently laid waste to Luna Park.

Above: The history of Coney Island in the twentieth century is also the history of destructive fires. Fire destroyed the original Steeplechase Park, Dreamland, and then, in 1944, Luna Park (shown here) ended up shutting down after flames ravaged most of its land. In addition, a number of other fires not connected to the amusement parks afflicted Coney Island throughout these years.

Above: In the years immediately after World War II, Coney Island beaches were crowded beyond imagination. This photo shows the mass of humanity that attempted to find a patch of sand on a summer day in 1948.

CHAPTER FOUR

Tides of Change

Coney Island After World War II

After struggling during the Depression and World War II, Coney Island bounced back with a vengeance in the late 1940s and early 1950s. On July 4, 1947, Coney Island registered its biggest day ever with 1.3 million visitors. The soldiers, sailors, and marines returning home contributed to the area's resurgence, and the general infusion of new money and disposable income helped stimulate Coney's economy and boost the prospects of its merchants. Steeplechase Park, now the only amusement park on the strip, rekindled its enormous popularity, with young men and women flocking there for many of the same reasons as the earlier generation. As Bill Feigenbaum—who grew up in Brooklyn in the 1950s and worked as a Steeplechase scooter boy— was quoted in *It Happened in Brooklyn*: "The whole idea of Steeple- chase was fun and sex. There was all that touching, hugging, falling down, bumping into each other, air ducts everywhere. When I worked at Steeplechase, I used to spend my whole lunch hour sitting in the audience watching the parade of people coming off the horse ride. And I was surprised to discover how many girls didn't wear panties."

The good times, however, were short-lived. By the late 1950s, Coney Island began to fall into a full-scale decline. Robert Moses, hostile to the cheap amusements from his first day as parks commis- sioner, ensured that the city did little to maintain this fun zone. In the eyes of many, his goal was to allow Coney Island to deteriorate to such an extent that it would encourage business flight and discourage visi- tors, thus making it an appropriate site for federally funded urban renewal. Urban renewal, or "urban removal" as its opponents called it, would, in effect, displace the community's least fortunate residents and totally destroy the community before federal funds could be secured to rebuild the area. Old-time merchants retired or sold their food concessions. Suburban flight, better roads, and widespread automobile ownership meant that many middle-class families who previously would have come to Coney Island now had the ability to choose from among many alternative places to spend their leisure time.

By the early 1960s, the development of low-income housing com- plexes led to an escalation in gang violence among the youth in the neighborhood. The old fun zone on the Bowery became a place full of crime, which instilled fear in would-be patrons. Hostility directed toward working-class white visitors and residents emerged as a major problem as black and Puerto Rican populations increased in the neighborhood. The 1964 race riots in Harlem and Bedford-Stuyvesant clearly also had an impact on the level of fear—residents and visitors were concerned that Coney Island might be next.

Then, on September 20, at the end of the 1964 season, Steeplechase Park closed its doors for good. Its closing ceremonies were attended by current and past employees and all surviving members of the Tilyou family—the family that had guided the operations of the "Funny Place" for more than sixty years. At the end of the closing ceremony, two bells tolled signaling the marking of time. Steeplechase, the simplest and oldest of the great Coney Island amusement parks, had outlasted the others, but it could not survive the wholesale decline of the neighborhood.

In the late 1960s and 1970s, Coney Island became a symbol of urban decay and decline. Generally seen as an impoverished neighborhood where drugs, crime, and hopelessness seemed to prevail, it was as if the local government had just given up on it. Nevertheless, New Yorkers, especially Brooklynites, never completely gave up on Coney Island. Even during the worst years, the beaches continued to be mobbed on hot summer weekends. Just as in the days of the Nickel Empire, people with limited economic means still sought out Coney's beaches and boardwalk for the refreshing sea breezes and the opportunity to take a swim in the cool, if not necessarily sparkling clean, Atlantic waters.

Below: Just try to find the sand in this mid-1940s photograph. Coney Island's attendance figures in the immediate post–World War II years were staggering.

In the last two decades of the twentieth century, Coney Island has experienced somewhat of an upturn. While the neighborhood continues to struggle with poverty, unemployment, and dilapidated housing, there have been signs of recovery as thousands of New Yorkers are rediscovering Coney's rich history. The renaissance of Brighton Beach to the east has helped to create an upturn in the prospects of its neighbor. So have the many outdoor concerts and the arrival of the Coney Island Cyclones, a minor league baseball team, and their new playing field, Keyspan Park. The legendary Cyclone roller coaster and Nathan's Famous hot dogs still attract scores of summer pleasure-seekers. The annual Mermaid Parade also pays homage to the carnivals, freak shows, and raucous street life of the Bowery as well as to the spirit of George Tilyou. And then there is the beach itself—beckoning new generations to experience Coney Island for themselves.

Above: Suzie, the girl from Germany with the elephant skin, is typical of the side-show performers featured on Coney Island's Bowery. Here, Suzie models for the crowd in 1944. In Coney Island today, there are two freak shows still operating, albeit on a much smaller and more toned-down scale.

Above: With Feltman's decline and closing in 1946, Nathan's was far and away the most popular eating establishment in Coney Island after World War II. By the mid-1950s, Nathan Handwerker had sold a hundred million hot dogs in his forty years of operation.

Above: Nathan Handwerker is shown in this 1966 photo passing the establishment that made him rich and famous. Handwerker retired to Sarasota, Florida, and died in 1994 at age eighty-three.

Above: Steeplechase Park persevered until 1964, even after Coney Island began to hit hard times. Here, two visitors to the Tilyou family's famed amusement park descend in the Parachute Jump high above the crowded beach on the Fourth of July, 1961.

Below: The 250-foot (76m)-high Parachute Jump in Steeplechase Park was a late addition to the park, purchased in 1941 from the New York World's Fair Lifesaver Exhibit. Passengers strapped themselves into canvas seats and were catapulted up to the top of the tower, slowly dropped into wide chutes, and then softly landed on rubber dampers. As another world war loomed on the horizon, this ride appealed to people's curiosity about soldiers jumping out of planes.

Below: Youth culture, especially aspects that featured socializing between the sexes, was a core component of Coney Island's appeal and one of its major selling points. Teenagers and young adults packed the beaches and amusement parks of the area during Coney's heyday—as they still do.

Opposite: The Cyclone never lost its luster—even as the rest of Coney Island fell into decline in the 1960s and 1970s. Perhaps this is partially a result of the incredible view it provides of the Atlantic Ocean and the Coney Island boardwalk, although more likely it is because people continue to want the minute and a half of heart-pounding terror as the Cyclone careens its way up, down, and around six turns at extraordinary speed.

Above: This 1951 image shows a Coney Island "girlie show," part of the carnival-like sideshows that were popular attractions in amusement parks for many years.

Left: Coney Island is most often thought of in association with youth culture. Here, however, a group of senior citizens takes a spin on the bicycle ride in Steeplechase's Pavilion of Fun during an outing in 1952. We have no idea, of course, whether they actually had fun or not.

Right: Whether or not their troop leader considered Steeplechase to be appropriate amusement, these four Girl Scouts seem to be enjoying the ride in this 1949 photograph. Notice Tilyou's trademark image—the smiling man with thirty-six teeth—prominently displayed on the ride.

Left: The Cyclone was one attraction that was able to maintain its popularity even through the hardest of times during the Great Depression, when this photo was taken, and into the 1960s and 1970s, when Coney Island fell into years of abandonment and decay.

Right: In the 1980s, the Cyclone was awarded official landmark status, meaning it will definitely be there for the next generation to enjoy. No matter what happens to the rest of Coney Island, there will be always be at least one reminder of the days when roller coasters were a novelty.

Opposite: Bundled up against the cold in December of 1959, three elderly women play a game of cards in front of a bathhouse on the Coney Island boardwalk. Rain or shine, summer or winter, Coney Island remains a place of recreation and entertainment for young and old alike.

Above: The Big Horn Ranch was an example of an attempt to bring Wild West atmosphere to Coney Island. Although the Big Horn Ranch is no longer standing, a wild and raucous atmosphere can still be found on Coney Island's Bowery.

Sources

BOOKS

Burrows, Edwin, and Mike Wallace. *Gotham: A History of New York City to 1898*. New York: Oxford University Press, 1999.

Frommer, Myrna Katz, and Harvey Frommer, editors. *It Happened in Brooklyn: An Oral History of Growing Up in the Borough in the 1940s, 1950s, and 1960s*. Orlando: Harcourt and Brace, 1993.

Glueck, Grace, and Paul Gardiner, editors. *Brooklyn: People and Places, Past and Present*. New York: Harry N. Abrams, Inc., 1991.

Kasson, John F. *Amusing the Million: Coney Island at the Turn of the Century*. New York: Hill and Wang, 1978.

McCullough, Edo. *Good Old Coney Island: A Sentimental Journey into the Past*. New York: Charles Scribner and Sons, 1957, 2000.

Nasaw, David. *Going Out: The Rise and Fall of Public Amusements*. New York: Harvard University Press, 1993.

Peiss, Kathy. *Cheap Amusements: Working Women and Leisure in Turn-of-the-Century New York*. Philadelphia: Temple University Press, 1986.

Wilensky, Elliott. *When Brooklyn Was the World, 1920–1957*. New York: Harmony Books, 1986.

The WPA Guide to New York City. New York: Random House, 1939, 1982.

WEBSITES

The American Experience Coney Island Enhanced Transcript (1990). PBS On-Line
www.pbs.org/wgbh/amex/coney/filmore/description.html

Aurbach, Laurence Jr. Coney Island: Forty Years as the Carnival Capital (1999).
http://users.erols.com/jaurbach/coney.htm

Sandy, Adam. Coney Island Pages (2001).
http://history.amusement-parks.com/users/adamsandy

Stanton, Jeffrey. Coney Island (1997).
http://naid.sppsr.ucla.edu/coneyisland/articles

Above: Proof positive that Coney Island was not just a summer place is found in this wonderful image of a crowd of people who, in February 1952, rented reclining chairs and sun reflectors by the hour in an attempt at winter sunbathing. Indoor tanning salons were, of course, still many years away.

Photo Credits

AP/ Wide World: pp. 109, 110, 111, 112–113, 117 top, 124–125

Brown Brothers: pp. 2–3, 6–7, 10–11, 18, 20 left, 24–25, 25 right, 28–29, 30–31, 33, 35, 38–39, 41, 42–43, 43 right, 44–45, 48–49, 49 bottom, 50, 51 top, 51 bottom, 52–53, 54, 55, 56–57, 58 left, 58–59, 62–63, 66–67, 68 left, 68–69, 70–71, 73, 74, 76 bottom, 76–77, 78 left, 78–79, 80–81, 86–87, 88–89, 90–91, 92–93, 94–95, 96, 100, 101, 102–103, 104 left, 104–105, 115, 118–119, 120

Corbis: pp. 12 left, 75, 84–85, 88 left, 93 right, 99 top, 108, 117 bottom, 121

Hulton/Archive: pp. 126–127

Museum of the City of New York: pp. 11 right, 22–23, 40 top, 40 bottom (Gift of M. M. Gordon), 46 top, 49 top, 53 bottom, 62 left, 65 top, 65 bottom, 67 right, 85 right, 106–107 (Gift of New York City Department of Parks), 113 right (Gift of New York Convention & Visitors Bureau), 122–123; ©J. H. Beal: pp. 26–27; The Byron Collection: pp. 16, 81 right, 82–83, 98; ©Samuel Gottscho, The Gottscho–Schleisner Collection: pp. 46 bottom, 47, 60–61; ©Hegger: pp. 20–21; ©Andrew Herman: pp. 12–13 (Gift of the Federal Arts Project, Works Project Administration); ©J. S. Johnston: pp. 14–15; The Leonard Hassam Bogart Collection: p. 8–9, 27 bottom, 37, 64 top, 64 bottom, ©Reginald Marsh: pp. 97 (Gift of Mrs. Felicia Meyer Marsh), 114 (Gift of Mrs. Felicia Meyer Marsh); ©Edward Roth: p. 116; ©Rudolph Simmon: p. 76 top (Gift of Kay Simmon Blumberg), 99 bottom (Gift of Kay Simmon Blumberg)

North Wind Picture Archives: p. 17

Above: From the proliferation of horse racing in the nineteenth century to the popularity of the Steeplechase ride in the twentieth century, Coney Island was once the center of equine entertainment. These children smile broadly as they careen around the bend on the Steeplechase ride, circa 1945.

Index